MW01126440

OREGON TRAIL JOURNAL OF

MEDOREM

CRAWFORD

An account of his trip across the plains
With the Oregon Pioneers of 1842

1897

Contents

BIOGRAPHICAL NOTES

When we consider today what the journey was like for the pioneers who migrated west in the mid-19th century, we wonder that anyone had the will and perseverance to make it. In fact, about 400,000 Americans crossed the perilous expanse of the Oregon Trail. This journal is the only record of one of the earliest large groups who made the trip.

When this company of pioneers set out, the 2,200-mile Oregon Trail was only recently being navigated by wagon trains. Up until 1840, it was only passable on foot or horseback. Medorem Crawford was typical of the travelers—young, intrepid, and with more grit than good sense—but he became one of Oregon's most important early settlers.

Medorem Crawford was born on June 24, 1819 in Orange County, New York to Samuel Gillespie Crawford and Elizabeth Davis. He was the eldest of six children and was 23 when he arrived in Oregon Territory in 1842.

By the 1850 federal census, he was married to Adeline Brown, with whom he had seven children. They were living in Oregon City, south of modern Portland, Oregon, and Medorem worked as a teamster. He at that time owned real estate worth $6,000 (about $180,000 in 2015 dollars). He was also serving in the territorial government.

He was a member of the Legislature of the Provisional Government of Oregon from 1847 to 1849. In 1860 he was elected to the State Legislature. He was held in high estimation by both U. S. Senators from Oregon, Baker* and Nesmith, as he was called to Washington to receive instructions for taking charge of escorting emigrants across the plains.

*Senator Edward Dickinson Baker (1811-1861) was such a close friend of Abraham Lincoln that Lincoln named his second son Edward Baker Lincoln (1846-1850). Though born in England, Edward Baker was a committed American citizen and a hero of the Mexican-American War. He became a Senator from Oregon in 1860 and worked with tireless devotion to keep the West Coast states in the Union. When war came, Baker kept his senate seat but formed a California regiment and led it in battle. On

October 21, 1861, Edward Dickinson Baker became the only sitting senator to be killed in battle in the Civil War.

He led the expeditions of 1861, '62 and '63 during the American Civil War. He was commissioned an officer in the U.S. Volunteers Quartermaster's Dept. Infantry Regiment on April 28, 1862 and mustered out on April 16 1864.

He was for all practical purposes in control of the first and, with rank of captain in the volunteer army, had command of the two succeeding. In 1864 Crawford was appointed collector of internal revenue for Oregon. His duties in this involved subjecting of the people to an unaccustomed form of taxation and the setting in order of a new system for raising revenue. He administered the duties of this office for five years. From 1871 to 1875 he was appraiser of customs at Portland.

The Crawfords moved fifty-five miles southwest to McMinnville and for a while worked a farm. They continued to prosper in the new Territory, and by 1870 they were living in Dayton, about 34 miles southwest of modern Portland, again farming, and with a personal estate reported at $8,252 ($150,000 in 2015 dollars) and real estate worth $17,000 (about $300,000 in 2015 dollars). Clearly the risk of migration was paying off for the Crawfords.

Adeline Crawford died May 20, 1879, and Medorem remarried the next year to Mrs. Eunice Burrows. In 1862, his son, Medorem Jr., had received an appointment to West Point, where he graduated in 1867. He was eventually promoted to Brigadier General and is buried at Arlington National Cemetery.

Medorem Crawford, Sr. died at his home near Dayton on December 26, 1891, at the age of 72. The *Morning Oregonian*, of Dec. 27, 1891, in commenting on his life says, "he was known to every person in Oregon during many years and remembered latterly by all who retained recollections of early days in Oregon. Medorem Crawford was a man to fix the impress of his individuality and character upon any community. As a pioneer he was among the most intelligent, far-seeing, and energetic, and as a State-builder, he bore a very important part."

1897 EDITORIAL NOTES

GENERAL:—

The printing and distribution of the primary sources of the history of the Pacific Northwest is calculated to promote the cause of the history in Oregon and throughout our country in several distinct and important directions. ,

Pioneers and their descendants will through this means be brought to an adequate appreciation of much valuable material not yet utilized. This will be preserved and rendered available to future generations of students.

The achievement of an intrepid, resolute, and capable people—the Oregon pioneers—will thus come to be truly and duly recognized.

A remarkable period of our country's expansion, one in which the national spirit was at its best, will be made instructive.

The youth of the Pacific Northwest must now draw his first historical inspiration from the exploits, struggles, and state building of men on the far away Atlantic seaboard, yet his own home section of the common country was the scene of deeds as heroic and effective, animated by motives even more youthful. The whole course of development from discovery and exploration to the establishment of a self-centered republic was accomplished here as well as there and independently. The scale was in miniature yet the results were substantial and far-reaching as they involved the destiny of the whole Coast and made us a truly continental nation facing both oceans.

These sources made accessible to the schools of the states of the Pacific Northwest will constitute a wealth of resources for historical parallels between the development of the east and the far west. The possibilities of historical instruction in American history in these schools will thus be revolutionized.

SPECIAL:—

This edition of this journal is not in popular form; it is primarily intended for the historical student. The original copy is followed

3

with verbal and literal exactness. The editor is under obligations to Mr. J. M. Crawford of Dayton, Yamhill county, Oregon, and Mrs. E. Stevens of Oregon City, Oregon, for the use of the original copy and for permission to contribute it to the searchers for original and indubitable historical evidence. The genuine historical student will have the tenderest appreciation of the adverse circumstances under which this record was made and be profoundly grateful that it was allowed to pass out of the family circle in this form for his use.

JOURNAL

March 17, 1842, Thursday-Left Havana 10 o'clock A. M. Left Salubria 4 past 12 o'clock on hoard Steam Boat Chemung for Geneva, landed near 5 o'clock P. M put up at the Washington Temperance house. Left for Rochester at 1/2 past 11, E. arrived at J past 4 in M., distance 50 miles, put up at the Eagle very much fatigued having had no rest last night. Left for Buffalo J past 8 M., arrd. y past 9 E., traviled by Rail road & Stage.

Saturday, March 19, find ourselves very sore & much fatigued. Lake full of ice no chance to get away today. Steam Boat Gen. Scot leaves a port about 12 miles down the Lake but we think it not advisable to go to it without a certainty of getting a passage.

The weather has been very fine since we started, roads very bad from Batavia to this place, distance 39 miles.

Sunday March 20, no prospect of getting away from this pi uncertain with regard to the best rout. Sunday forenoon, attended church, in the evening heard a lecture from Doct. White on the Oregon subject.

Monday 21, heavy east & north-east wind and considerable snow, cold windy stormy night.

Tuesday 22d, morning stormy, north-east wind, 2 or 3 inch, snow, very unpleasant indeed. Left Buffalo at 11 o'clock in the morning in a lumber waggon on our way to the Steam Boat. Arrived at Cattaragus Creek past 10 evening, roads in a most horrible condition distance from Buffalo 30 miles. Left for Erie on board Steam Boat Erie at J past 10 o'clock.

Wednesday 23d morning, arrived after a very pleasant ride at 7 o'clock evening, put up at the American Hotel in Erie good accommodations.

Erie is a very pleasat and interesting place, has a fine harbor, is well laid out and has a public square and most splendid buildings. Left Erie for Pittsburgh Thursday, 24th, morning J past 11 o'clock. Friday morning 7 o'clock stopped to breakfast at Georgetown 52 miles from Erie. Traviled the last, 15 miles in a covered waggon, roads quite bad. Called at Mercer a pleasant village 66 miles south of Erie, wether cloudy & freqent showers but warm. Saturday 26, morning, stopped for breakfast 12 miles from Pittsburgh, rode all night in a covered waggon, bad roads, arrived at Pittsburgh on Saturday I o'clock P. M., almost, tiered to death having had no rest since we left Erie. Do not like the looks of Pittsburgh at all. The city is badly laid out, streets are narrow and dirty and the houses nil smoked with coal. Left Pittsburgh on board S. B. Westpoint for Cincinnati at J past 7 evening.

Waked up in the morning some rested found ourselves in Virginia. Called at Wheeling 3 hours on Sunday morning, March 27. Wheeling has the appearance of a business place but like Pittsburgh its buildings are covered with the smoke of Pit coal. Called at Marietta a few minutes; very pretty place. Monday 28 March, nothing of particular interest has occurred today. The weather is remarkable fine, the forest trees along the river are covered with green leaves and the peach trees all in blossom. Passed the state line between Virginia & Kentucky about noon very little of the country to be seen from the river a range of hills bordering on each side only an occasional farm on either side between the river and the hill.' Passed several rafts today and met steamboats. Landed and reed. 2 passengers at Portsmouth one of the most splendid villages I ever saw at the termination of the Ohio Canal.

Arrived at Cincinnati about midnight Left the boat at 6 o'clock on Tuesday morning. Took breakfast at a tavern, went about the city, found Col. John White, had a very polite invitation to stop at his house while we stayed in the City accepted the invitation & stayed to dinner after dinner Col went round the City and introduced us to some of the first men of the City. We were very kindly treated indeed & had many warm invitations to call and stay the evening. March 28 the weather is uncomfortable warm.

Saturday April 2, Left Cincinnati for St. Louis past 3 o'clock P. M. about 5 o'clock we had a fair view of Gen. Wm. H. Harrison's residence and tomb the scene was a most beautiful one, the house in which he lived is very pleasantly situated some 30 rods from the river, it is surrounded with green trees &c. The tomb is on the top of a beautiful knoll surrounded by a very handsome fence containing probably about 6 or 8 acres. The country along the river particularly on the Ohio side is a beautiful and apparently level & rich section.

Spent the Sabbath in Louisville, Kentucky. Took our horses ashore and rode back in the country & was very much pleased with the fine dwellings, gardens, & farms &c. Attended the Presbyterian Church in the afternoon & the Methodist in the evening—both were interesting.

Monday morning quite unwell taken with a diaerea eat no breakfast & very little dinner, took some Brandy & sugar and soon felt better. Left Louisville near 5 o'clock P. M. passed over the falls in safty stopt at New Albany Indiana small but pleasant place. Tuesday called at several small places along the river the most delightful weather I ever saw.

Wednesday April fi, rainy & cloudy passed Caro at mouth of the Ohio entered the Mississippi at 7 o'clock A. M. Cairo is a miserable looking place, said to be unhealthy.

A severe thunder storm after night Boat obliged to stop on account of darkness, started some time before morning, ran on a snag and injured the wheel some, soon repd. & started again Thursday fine morning after the storm—a very warm sun.

Arrived at St. Louis past 4 P. M. putup at the St. Louis Exchange. Friday & Saturday spent my time riding about the city & visiting my fellow passengers on board the Neptune especially Misses Wells & Marshall.

Sunday April 10, very hot indeed rode out to the Prairie Hotel parted with Mr. Beebe of New York who I first met at Pittsburgh.

Monday spent this day in a most agreeable manner with Mr. Sublett who has spent several years in the mountains.

Spent ten days here in St. Louis very agreeably up to Monday, April 18. Esqr. Crocker, Alex. & John started for Independence by land taking 0 mules & 3 horses. Reed a letter this morning from

Father & Sister. After having spent 2 weeks in St. Louis and having formed several very agreeable acquaintances we left Thursday 21 April at 8 o'clock evening for Independence on S. B. Rowena. Friday extremely hot. Called at Jefferson City 7 o'clock evening.

April 24, Sunday morning 10 o'clock cannot get over the bar. Heavy rain in the evening. Monday morning 9 o'clock got over the bar; a very cold wind. Called at Lexington 2 hours at noon 8 couple of Gentlemen and Ladies & band of music came on bord for a pleasure party. Spent the evening very pleasantly in conversation and dancing with the Ladies. Tuesday morning very fine weather. Called at Liberty landing 4 hours visited the Arsenal at Liberty village 3 miles from the river. 16 couple of Gent and Ladies came on board. Left the S. boat at 2 o'clock arr'd at Independence at 3 found the Boys had arrived the night before. On Friday April 29, we pitched our tent and turned our animals out in the Prairie about 6 miles from Independence we got our supper and slept in the tent. Saturday we got out all our things from the village. Sunday May first we spent all this day in the camp.

May 2d a meeting of all who are bound to Oregon was called to decide whether to wait for a company from Platt; Decided to wait 12 days. 4th Left camp 10 o'clock M. stopped at 2 o'clock to dinner. Started at 4 o'clock, E. stopped at 6 o'clock pitched our tent in a fine spot traveled 12 miles today, had a heavy frost last night ruined most of the corn and fruit in this country.

Rode to Independence from camp 18 M. 7, Returned, 3 more waggons came to camp. May 8, Sunday went to Shawnee meeting, returned by way of Mission. 10 Uncommon dry an hot, no rain since we came to camp. 12, went to Independence, a fine shower. 14, Doctor came to camp with 36 Cattle. 16 Left camp at I o'clock E. drove 15 mi and camped at 7 o'c. E. on the Santafe rout, found water pleanty, wood & pasture scarce.

In our company were 16 waggons & 105 persons including children &: 51 men over 18 years of age. 17. Started at 9 o'c. M. detained J hour by losing the trail. Left the Santa Fee trail at 2 o'c and camped at J past 3 evening, weather very warm. Traviled about 12 miles. I more wagon and 3 men came on.

A violent rain this morning much excitement in camp about Dogs: 22 dogs shot, stopped raining 9 o'c.

May 18, Started at I o'clock E. without a track endeavoring to find the right trail. Camped on the right trail at 7 o'c. E. Traviled 10 miles.

A severe rain this morning; laid out and got very wet. Started at 4 past 9 M. detained by crossing 2 creeks stopped at 2 E. traviled 5 miles.

Very heavy rain last night & cloudy this morning. Moved camp about one mile. All gone ahead except 3 wagons w ho are detained with a sick child.

Another rainy night & cloudy cold & uncomfortable morning. Mrs. Lancaster's only child a daughter 16 months old died 10 o'clock M. the Doctor called the disease symptomatick fever accompanied with worms. Continues to rain moderately. May 21. After burying the child we started and drove 6 miles.

22d Sunday started at 7 o'clock M. and drove 25 miles over a beautiful country; camped in good season. 23d Some rain last night & cloudy cool morning. Started at 9 o'clock M. drove to the Kansas river and crossed with safty, Distance 10 miles. 24. Stopped today to repair waggons.

25. Started at 4 o'clock E. drove 6 miles camped at 7 o'clock E. part of the company still ahead. 26. Started at 7o'clock M. considerable rain, overtook company at 2 o'clock, took dinner and all started together. Camped on Vermillion Creek at 7 o'clock E. traviled 18 miles.

May 27. Mrs. Lancaster very sick & unable to trnvil. Part, of the company unwilling to wait 5went on, much dissatisfaction in the camp. Capt. White rode on and found the company about 8 miles ahead they agreed to wait until Sunday morning for Mr. Lancaster. The weather is very fine and the country around delightful.

Rainy morning, Mrs. Lancaster some better. Started at 4 past 9 oc. M. Cleared off warm, arrived at camp J p. 4 o'clock E. traviled 8 miles, weather very hot.

Sunday Mrs. Lancaster is very low, much dissatisfaction in the camp, some want to go on and some want to stay. 3 wagons went on 2 miles, a very warm day. 30 All the wagons except Mr. Lancaster started at J past 6 o'clock M. cool wind. 30th May Mr. Lancaster concluded to take his wife back. Capt. White and others accompany him to the K river. Stopped to dinner 14 hours. Camped at £ past 6 o'clock E. traviled 20 miles. 31. Started at 4 past 5 oc. M. Stopped 24 hours for dinner, camped on Blue River at4o'clock E. traviled 15 miles; most splendid spring water there, met 4 waggons from the Mountains, 3 o'clock.

June 1st Started at £ 5 M. commenced raining at 6 stopped 3 hours, went on after the rain ceased. Stopped 2 hours for dinner. Camped at 5 o'clock E. traviled 10 miles. Doct. White overtook us at 4 o'clock E.

2d. Tremendous rain & wind last night. Commenced standing guard last night. Cold wind & disagreeable morning. Started at I o'clock E. Camped at 7. E. traviled 8 miles.

June 3d The company started at 5 oclock M. & left myself ■with 3 others to wait for Mr. Burns and others who were detained by Mr. Lancaster.

4. Started at G o'clock M. intending to go back to the Blue River & there stay for Mr. Burns. Met Mr. Burns & his company together with O'Fallen 2 miles back, turned & came on with them. Stopped 2 hours for dinner. Camped at 6 o'clock, E. traviled 22 miles. Cold wind. 5. Sunday, Started at 6 o'clock M. Stopped 1J hours for dinner, overtook the company. Camped on the Blue at J past 4 o'clock E. traviled 21 miles.

G. All started together at 7 o'clock M. commenced raining at 9, camped at 10, rain ceased, took dinner and started at I o'clock. Camped at 6 o'clock E. traviled 16 miles rainy night.

June, cold, damp, & disagreeable morning rained until 10 o'clock M. Started at J past I o'clock, camped at past G o'clock E. traviled 10 miles.

Cloudy morning started at £ past 7 o'clock. Stopped for dinner at p. 11: started at p. 2. Camped at 7 o'clock E. on the head waters of the Blue R. which we have been following up for the last 3 days, good water & wood, traviled 16 miles.

Left Blue R. at 6 o'clock M. Crossed the Pawnee Trail at 8 o'clock. Stopped at •§ p. 12 for dinner without wood or water except what we carried with us. Started at 2 o'clock & traviled through a ridge of country destitute of wood & water. Camped at 7 o'clock E. on the Platte R. traviled 25 miles.

June 10. Started at 8 o'clock M. & followed up the Platte R. Stopped for dinner at £ past 12, started at 2. Camped at 5 o'clock E. traviled 12 miles.

June 11. Difficulty between Doct. White & John Force. Started at 8 o'clock M. stopped for dinner 2 hours, camped at 5 o'clock E. traviled 10 miles. 12. Sunday, Started at 7 o'clock M. Stopped at 12, found a band of Buffalo near the camp nearly 100 killed 3 very good Bulls. Started at 3, saw many Buffalo. Camped at 6 o'clock E. traviled 14 miles. Buffalo came close around the camp killed 6.

June 13. Large herds of Buffalo in plain sight around the camp. Started in good season. Saw thousands of Buffalo traviled 15 miles, little feed for horses.

June 14. Our animals alarmed last night by the Buffalo approaching the camp. 2 oxen shot by the Guard through mistake but neither of them killed. Started at 8 o'clock M. Commenced raining at J p. 11. Stopped for dinner at 12. Started at £ p. 2. Camped 18 miles. started at 7 o'clock M. Saw thousands of Buffalo near the trail stopped for dinner at 1/2 p. 11, good wood and pasture, but poor water, very warm day.

The month for which Capt. White was elected being up the company elected Mr. Hastings by a majority of 12 over Mr. Meek. Concluded not to move camp today, traviled 9 miles.

Remain in camp today to wash our clothes.

June 16. More difficulty and misunderstanding in the company. Doct. White with a few others concluded to leave.

Rain this morning. The majority of the company started at 8 o'clock under Capt. Hastings. Two waggons and 13 men remained Capt. Fallen. Started at 11 o'clock passed the other party and camped at 6 o'clock. They passed us again and camped 3 miles ahead, we traviled 14 miles, quite cold.

Started at 7 o'clock. Cold wind & extremely uncomfortable. Commenced to rain at 10 o'clock stopped. Started at 2 camped at 7 on the South fork of Platte traviled 18 miles. Capt.

2 miles ahead. For 2 days we have seen no Buffalo. Capt. Fallen brought us some meat.

June 19. Sunday, Started at 7, stopped for dinner 2£ hours within I mile of Capt. Hastings. Camped on the Platte within mile of the other company at 6, traviled 20 miles.

Capt. Hastings & comp, crossed over the river & we followed immediately.

The South Fork where we crossed is mile wide but not deep the bottom is quick sand. Left the South Fork and took N. V. [direction] for the N. Fork. The other company went south of us. Camped on the North Fork. The other company 2 miles behind, traviled 15 M.

Started early and kept up the River good road in the forenoon. Stopped 3 hours for dinner, several hunters from the other company took dinner with us, some hills to cross Camped early traviled 20 miles.

Started early, good road. 3 men left the other Company for Fort Laromie [Laramie] took dinner with ns.

Capt. Fallen & Esq. Crocker went on to Fort L. very warm. Camped early traviled 20 miles. Mosketoes pleanty.

Started early, kept along the river, water good. Saw some boatmen from the Fort stoppod 3 hours for dinner. Camped early traviled 10 miles.

Started early drove very fast stopped for dinner nearly opposite the Chimney* a very remarkable mound rising like a pyramid some 100 feet and then a perpendicular column standing on the top probably 200 feet high. Saw a Buffalo crossing the River, Chaised him back to the hills. The most remarkable thing I have seen is the deception in distances. Bluffs which appear within I mile are often 5 miles from us. Camped early traviled 20 miles.

*Chimney Rock

June 25. Started 7. Cattle's feet very sore traviled slow. River bottom 3 to 5 miles wide, stopped for dinner 4 hours, very hot, left the River traviled 12 miles. Camped without water or wood in a valley bordered on each side by high Bluffs presenting the most romantic scenery T ever saw.

June 26. Sunday, Started early without breakfast came to good wood and water at 8 o'clock. Camped on the side of a hill in a grove. Started at I o'clock saw the other company coming on, drove to Horse Creek camped traviled 14 miles. Horses very much frightened about midnight nearly all broke lose.

Started at 4 o'clock without breakfast stopped on the

River at 10 J o'clock. Started at I o'clock very sultry day. Cattle very near giving out. Camped at sundown, traviled 18 miles.

Started late drove to the Forts by noon, traviled 10 miles. Found 2 Forts with several men at each whose business it is to trade with the Indians. Capt. H came up, 5 o'clock.

Preparing carts & disposing of our cattle in order to expedite our journey.

Very busy preparing to start tomorrow. July 1. Difficulty between Doct. White and Capt. Fallen. Fallen refused to go with us. Remained here all day. 2d joined the other company under Capt. Hastings. Started at 9 o'clock met a company from the mountains near the Fort. Camped at five, good wood and water poor grass, traviled 12 miles through a hilly and barren country.

July 3. Sunday Entered what is called the Black Hills. Traviled 15 miles over bad road without seeing water. Mr. Fitch Patrick employed as guide came to camp.

4th. Waggon to repair. Wrote a few lines to my Parents. Started at noon had a very rough road. Came to water 6J o'clock, traviled 11 miles. Cart broke down 2 miles from camp.

5. Repaired the cart. Started at noon found good water at three o'clock, had some heavy hills to rise. Buffalo very scarce. Camped early good wood, water and grass, traviled 9 miles.

G. Started at six drove on at a good pace until noon found a first rate camping place. Concluded to remain here today as there was no good chance ahead, traviled 12 miles.

July 7. Started early traveled over a rough mountainous & barren country found no good camping place until late afternoon traviled 16 miles, found a fine band of Buffalo cows.

Started at 8 o'clock had a very hilly road stopped for dinner at 12 o'clock on creek started at 4 camped on the Platte, good wood and water but short grass, travlied 15 miles.

Started at 7 o'clock stopped at 9 on Deer Creek. Second trial of Mr. Moss for not standing guard. Jury could not agree. Started at 2 camped at 7, traviled 15 miles. Saw several bands of fine Buffalo cows our hunter killed one I think decidedly the best meat I ever eat.

Sunday Started at 7 very heavy west wind yesterday & today.

July 10. Sunday, Crossed over the Platte & camped traviled miles. 11. Started at 8, left the Platte & Black Hills traviled miles over hilly roads & camped in sight of the Red Buttes good water and grass but no wood. Cool wind.

Started in good season saw an abundance of Buffalo crossed some very Rocky Hills said to be the commencement of the Mountains. Stopped for dinner 2 hours. Camped in a little valley surrounded with bushes grass good & first rate water and wood, traviled 16 miles.

Very cold, water in a pail froze ice like thick window glass. Started early raized a long hill detained by wagons breaking down I hour.

July 13. Stopped for late dinner on very warm road level and sandy not a particle of grass, passed beds of white substance partaking of the nature of salt and magnetia &c. Camped at sunset on Sweet Water, traviled 20 m. Baily shot while walking through camp by accidental discharge of a gun from a waggon, he lived about one hour.

July 14. Buried Baily near Independence Rock J mile from camp. My feelings on this occasion can hardly be described. A young man in the vigor of youth and health taken from our company wrapped in a Buffalo Robe & and buried in this dismal Prairie. What sad tidings for his Parents & friends who like my own are far from here. Went out hunting Buffalo.

July 15. Bayed about 15 miles from camp last night in company with three others. Killed a Bull and as we had eaten nothing since we left camp we soon built a fire and roasted some meat, killed a cow about 11 o'clock, got into camp towards night found all the rest of the company had more meat than us. Today Capt. Hastings month being up himself and Lieu Lovejoy were re-elected. 16 Concluded to move camp nearer to the Buffalo. Started at 8 o'clock followed up the Sweet Water at the foot of a tremendous mountain composed of solid rock. Sweet water passes through a gap in this mountain, great curiosity.

July 16. Camped on Sweet water at 3 o'clock. Went with 2 others about 1 mile from camp and ascended the mountain after having viewed the rock we decended about half way when we discovered a party of 200 Indians approaching camp.

Made all possible haste to camp. Indians met us but let ns pass. Found they had taken our Capt. & Lieu, prisoners at the Independence Rock where they had been taking observations and brought them to camp. Showed no hostility. Presented them with tobaco. Camped near us, traviled 12 miles. 17. Sunday After calling

15

on us & receiving some ammunition they left & traviled up the River. We stay to make meat. Very warm. Several men gone hunting. Very difficult to get meat.

Mr. Bennitt's Daughter slightly wounded by an accidental discharge of a gun.

Monday July 18. We reluctantly remained here today. Several gone hunting slight shower of rain. Considerable of meat brought in today.

Started at7£ o'clock followed up the Sweet Water, tremendous Rocky Mountains on each side. Camped at 12| o'clock, good grass, water and wood, traviled 7 miles.

Stay here today to dry what meat we have and get more. Hunters driven into camp by the Indians who are scattered in small parties all around us. Indians take 2 horses from Binnit's son & Weston. They came to camp very much frightened. Capt several others went out to see if they had any of our men several of whom were out yet. All came in safe. False alarm in the night.

Thursday, July 21. Stay here all this day Brown lost a horse leg broke by a kick. Indians came back before noon a few came near camp & told many different stories. We observed they had more horses than when they went up. 280 were counted in their Party. They passed quietly by and said they were going home. Extremely warm.

22. Started at 7, traviled on at a good pace until 10 met a party of Shian [Cheyenne] Indians. Camped within two miles of their Village, about noon the Chiefs together with some hundreds of others came to camp. We made them presents of ammunition, tobaco &c. and smoked with them. Started after dinner passed their village which consisted of several hundred lodges.

Friday 22d July. Several Indians accompanied us to camp. Mr. Fitch Patrick judged they were in the village of Crows, Shians, & Sues between 4 & 5000. Many of our Company traded horses with them. Camped near sun set on Sweet Water, traviled 15 m.

23 Started at 7-J o'clock, bad road. Crossed the Sweet Water a number of times, some very narrow passes between the mountains. Camped on S. W. at noon, traviled 7 miles a small party of Indians came to camp, about 100 more Indians came to camp at 2 o'clock. They were a war party of Sues & Shians who had been to fight the Snakes. They returned as usual in several parties another small party came up near night. A few came to camp to smoke.

Sunday 24. Started early left the creek & traviled over a hill of sand without a particle of grass ground covered with wild sage. Saw mountains with snowy sides far to the N. W. struck Sweet Water about noon stopped for dinner 2 hours crossed the creek several times afternoon. Camped on the creek good wood and grass traviled 15 miles.

25 Started 6£ o'clock rose a long hill came on the creek & camped at 11 for dinner drove two hours afternoon camped on the creek much the best grass we have seen since we left the Fort good spring water & pleanty of wood traviled 12 miles. Wild geese for several days have been frequently seen & fish are caught from Sweet Water creek.

Tuesday 26, July. The nights are astonishingly cold & the days are very warm. Last night I lay under a thick Blanket & Buffalo Robe with my clothes on. Started early traviled over a long rocky hill camped at noon, got already to start after dinner and a waggon broke down stay here tonight, traviled 10 miles had a severe cold rain.

Started early stopped a short time for dinner. Camped near sun set on Sweet Water, traviled 16 miles.

Started 7 o'clock left Sweet Water crossed the dividing ridge. Camped at 10 o'clock on a little stream running westward, traviled 6 miles. Left the cart here, one waggon left. Snowy mountains constantly in sight.

Friday 29. Started 7 o'clock traviled over a sandy barren country destitute of game & every thing but wild sage, high mountains north of us apparently 20 or 30 miles covered with snow. Camped after noon on Little Sandy Creek which empties in Green River a very pretty stream but much warmer than I expected traveled 14 miles.

Started early stopped on the creek for dinner 2 hours. Camped near sun set on Big Sandy Creek traveled 20 miles.

Sunday. Rainy morning Started 7. Commenced raining very cold & unpleasant. Considerable decending ground. Camped on the creek at 3 o'clock traviled 15 miles. Much talk about dividing the company at Green River.

August 1. Monday started at 7. Commenced raining soon rained moderately crossed Green River and camped 11 o'clock traviled 6 miles. Some of the company preparing to pack from here rainy afternoon and evening. 2d. Cold wet morning some making pack saddles and others repairing their waggons determined to take them through.

Capt. Hastings with 8 waggons started at 8 o'clock, Meek Pilot. The best wagons were taken on 2 were left standing the rest destroyed to repair others. In our camp there is 27 men, Mr. Fitchpatrick Captain and Pilot. Finished making packsaddles cashed goods and preparing to start tomorrow.

Thursday Aug. 4. All started with pack animals at 8 o'clock had very little trouble on the way arrived at Ham's Fork of Green River at 4 o'clock. Camped good grass and wood traviled 20 miles in a different direction from that which the waggons took. We saw high mountains covered with snow to the south west.

Started at 7, saw some of Capt. H. company the waggons camped 2 miles behind us last night. Said they had to leave one waggon the first day. Stopped early for dinner cashed liquor. Started & crossed a considerable hill cold and rainy afternoon got very wet, rain ceased and we camped 5 o'clock on the same creek traviled 18 miles.

Saturday Aug. 6. Started early traviled 6 hours before dinner over a very rough mountainous country in some places we were obliged to all follow one path. Camped near sunset on the same creek good grass little wood, Traviled 22 miles.

7. Started in good season followed up the creek some time crossed a hill to the north commenced raining crossed some very bad water courses. Stopped for dinner at the side of a high mountain rain stopped started soon, rain and hail. Crossed two tremendous mountains and camped on Bear River near sunset traveled 25 miles. Saw a very large Indian trail nearly fresh. The river runs nearly north here.

Monday Aug. 8. Started as usual followed down the River level road very high mountain on each side of the River Bottom which is better soil than we have seen for some time. Stopped on the River a short time for dinner. Two accidents this afternoon by falling from horses not serious. A few trout caught from the river Today. Traveled 20 miles and camped on Tommaux Fork.

9. Started early across the Fork and crossed over a tremendour mountain and stopped for dinner on the river, had level road this afternoon. Camped in good season on Tullock's Fork a Branch running from the Mountains into the River traviled 18 miles..

Wednesday Aug. 10. Saw fresh sines of Indians started early. Indians soon came to us. They were Ponarchs and moving in the same direction with us many of them traviled with us until 3 o'clock when we struck the river and camped, traveled 16 miles. Several horses were procured from them on reasonable terms by our company. Their whole company soon came up and camped near us.

Some trading this morning started at 8J o'clock left the river before noon saw some of the finest springs of water which form a large creek. Saw the soda springs and Boiling springs the greatest Natural Curiosity I ever saw. Camped near soda springs good place traviled 15 miles. Some Indians came to camp.

Friday Aug. 12. Went to see the Boiling springs again this morning the hole through which the water spouts is about I foot in diameter the water which kept a continual Boiling rises frequently to the hight of 3 feet. It is said at times to rise much higher. It is Blood warm and has a sulphur and mineral taste there appears to be a species of Rock constantly forming around the hole which is already considerably elevated. There is a smaller hole near which appears to serve as a vent through which the air is constantly circulating. Started 7, a few Indians in camp 2 of our company started ahead for Fort Hall. Saw a singular spring partaking considerably of the quallities of soda.

Friday Aug. 12. Stopped for dinner about 2 o'clock. Started soon camped on Portnough traviled 23 miles.

13. Horses strayed off some distance from camp started in good season stopped early for dinner drove on again until near sunset and camped 011 Ross Fork in deep valley on a beautiful little stream traviled 25 miles. 14. Sunday. Started in good season and traviled very fast in order to get to the Fort early as possible. Stopped for dinner on Ross Fork. Some Fort men came to camp started and crossed several spring Brooks camped 011 Snake or Lewis River near Fort Hall traviled 25 miles. 15. visited the Fort found it much smaller than Laramie but very well conducted. Commenced writing a letter.

Tuesday 16. Finished my letter to my Parents. Visited the Fort. 17. Concluded not to start today. Wrote to W. C. Enos of St. Louis. Capt. H. with seven waggons came in. 18. Starting is again deferred until tomorrow. 19. Started about 9 o'clock kept down the River. Crossed several marshy places, very warm day and much trouble with packs. Camped on the River, traviled 15 miles. 20. Started in good season saw the American falls. It is not a perpendicular fall but more like rapids interspersed with large rocks. Met a large number of Indians. Doct went back and traded fish and horse from them stopped for dinner in a very bad place. Doct came up started camped on river traviled 12 miles.

Aug. 21. Sunday. Concluded to wait for the Company as some are not satisfied to go without a Pilot. Company passed about I o'clock. We packed up and started found them Camped about three miles on the River. Mr. McDonald came up soon. 22d Started without breakfast and traviled very fast until 8 o'clock stopped on a creek three hours. Started and drove on a trot nearly all day, very rocky hard for horses feet. The same Barren Country covered with sage continues. Camped on a Little Brook at 5 o'clock traviled 30 m good water and grass, little wood suffered very much with dust.

Tuesday 23d Aug. Started early drove fast. Came close to the river camped at 10 on Goose Creek. H. B. Company arrived 1J hours before us our cattle very much fatigued concluded not to try to keep up with the H. B. Company with our cattle. Company started two hours before us we drove moderately camped early traveled 20 miles. Doct. White left us for the H. B. Company whom he intends to go with to Fort Vancouver. Only 8 men left in our Company without a Pilot. 24. Started in good season and traviled moderately, fine cool day camped about noon. Giger and others passed with many animals. Started at 2J o'clock. Camped on a very pretty Brook traviled 18 miles. Tuesday Aug. 25. Started at 7-1/2 crossed two deep ravines, very rocky, passed an old camping gr[oun]d at 10 1/2 o'clock concluded not to stop drove on at a good pace decended into a tremendous valley with banks of perpendicular rock at least 200 feet high on the north side a large portion of water issues out of the rock nearly half way up. Camped at 3J o'clock on a large stream formed mostly by springs of the above description, traviled 21 miles.

Started at 7, kept down the Creek which is very rapid left the Creek and decended a steep hill. Crossed a beautiful stream. Camped at 11. Started at 2 passed some Indian Lodges traded fish both fresh and dry left the river rose a tremendous hill travellid on till dark no appearance of water very dark until 9 when the moon arose decended a tremendous hill found the river we left and camped at 10 o'clock night in a miserable sandy and rocky place traviled 30 M.

Saturday. Started at 8 kept down the river on the side of a steep bank where we were obliged to all follow one narrow path cross some steep ravines camped at 12 on an island in Snake river good grass concluded to stay here today and let our animals recruit, traviled 10 M.

Started early kept down the river along a steep side-hill saw many Indians who live along the river and subsist principally on fish traded fresh fish from them. Sunday 28, Aug. Camped 11-1/2 for dinner several Indians in camp. Left the river for a short time after dinner saw large sandbanks drifted like snow. Camped on a slew of the river very high grass, trav. 18 M. horses got frightened and ran some distance from camp, probably wolves.

Started at 7, cold morning followed down the river awhile left the river very barren country less sage than formerly. Crossed a large branch followed it through a tremendous gap in the mountain for at least two miles the rock standing up on each side probably 200 ft. Camped for dinner at the River many Lodges near several came into camp. 29. Followed down the river after dinner crossed On to an Island & camped near sunset, trav. 20 M.

Started at 7 kept down the River a short time took dinner on a small Branch very poor grass. Find the country growing more barren not even producing sage. Camped near sunset on a beautiful little Branch in a valley surrounded on three sides by high hills traveled 18 miles.

Followed down the Branch to the river about I miles in search of the horses, found the River as well as the Branch flowing among high cliffs of rock with scarcely room for a path on its Banks. 31st Aug. Started at 7J rose a long hill astonishingly barren country decended to the river stopped for dinner tolerable good grass, found Indians pleanty towards evening. Camped near their village poor grass trav. 18. M.

Thursday Sept. 1st, 1842. Many Indians come to camp traded pleanty of fish started 8, crossed 2 small streams which are said to be hot water. It was discovered by some of our party attempting to drink they said the water burned their hands took dinner on the on the river very warm day poor grass. Camped on the river poor grass traviled 15 miles.

Friday Sept. 2d. Started at 8-1/2 no alteration in the general appearance of the country took dinner on the river very poor grass Camped in the evening on Warior River a Branch of the Snake traviled 14 miles.

3d. Started 7-1/2 crossed W. R. arrived at Fort Boyzea [Boise] at 9. Crossed over Snake River in a Canoe to the Fort which stands on the north side of the river procured some provisions. Crossed back traviled down the river a short distance & camped for dinner. Fort B. is a new Establishment. It has been a short time in operation but is not yet completed. We saw but one white man who was French. The company left the Fort on Thursday.

Sept. 3d. At the Fort we tasted musk mellon but of a very indifferent quallity. They raise corn & a few other vegetables in small quantities. From the fort we saw a large smoke at a distance supposed to proceed from a volcanick mountain. Left camp at 11 o'clock & traveled briskly over a sandy country suffered considerable for water as the day was exceedingly hot came to a creek about 6 oclock & never was water to me more exceptable though of a very indifferent quality, passed down the Creek a short distance at the foot of a mountain & found boiling water running out of the ground. It made its appearance just above the age of the water in the River in a Boiling state for over a hundred yards it runs more or less. One of our company cooked a fish which he caught from the creek in about two minutes perfectly through. The water was so salt that the fish was sufficiently seasoned. Crossed the Creek & camped common grass traveled 15 m.

Concluded to stay here & let our cattle & horses rest today. Two of our company getting impatient left us this morning spent the day repairing, washing, &c.

Monday 5th Sept. Started at 7-1/2 oclock left the Creek our road led mostly through vallies we found more grass & and less sage than common came to a little water at 10 o'clock but concluded not to stop. Exceedingly warm came to a small stream at 2 oclock & camped. Cattle far behind & much fatigued traveled 16 m.

Started at 7-1/2 followed down the stream found Snake River close by followed it down about one mile & struck across a mountain, Came to a creek at 10 oclock. Stopped for dinner 3 hours our path wound along the sides of mountains & frightful precipices & in many places if our animals make one miss-step it would be certain death. The path continued up & down rocky hills until we came to a good camping ground about 5 oclock traviled 13 m.

Started at 7-1/2 rose a most tremendous hill the highest I have rose on the rout, got a fall from a horse hurt my foot some. The road is more precipitous than ever, up & down and constantly over rocks. Crossed several streams. Stopped for dinner at 10 oclock started at 1, and commenced climbing hills again crossed several small streams and found good grass most of the way came to the stream on which we camped last night. Camped at 4 oc traviled 10 miles.

Thursday 8, Sept. Horses strayed far from camp and instead of an early start as we intended we got off at 9 oclock we left the Branch and gradually a rose a long hill. Stopped for dinner on a small stream at 12 oclock started at 2-1/2 & continued to rise by degrees.

The country over which we have traviled to day is mostly covered with Bunch Grass which the Horses are very fond of. Wo at last found the top of the mountain at a distance we could see what we suppose to be the Blue mountains and they struck us with terror their lofty peaks seemed a resting place for the clouds. Below us was a large plain and at some distance we could discover a tree which we at once recognized as "the lone tree" of which we had before heard. We made all possible speed and at o'clock the advance party arrived at the Tree nearly an hour before the cattle. The Tree is a large Pine standing in the midst of an immense plain intirely alone. It presented a truly singular appearance and I believe is respected by every traviler through this almost Treeless Country. Within a few yards we found pleanty of water and we soon made ourselves comfortable by a good fire. As soon as we arrived at the top of the hill in sight of the Blue mountains felt an uncommon chilly wind which increased so as to be uncomfortable before we arrived. As soon as we reached the valley we found our old friend Sage flourishing in a most unwelcome manner. The grass about camp was not good, traviled 18 miles.

Friday 9. Sept. Horses far from camp this morning, found pleanty of frost on our beds and all about. Left camp at 8 oclock but was a long time finding the right trail. Cold wind from the B, mountains on tops of which we soon discovered heaps of snow.

Came to a large Creek which we followed a while stopped for dinner at 12-1/2 oclock. Started at 3 crossed the Creek. Crossed 2 more creeks soon and camped at oclock. We should have traviled on but we was afraid of being in the night without water, this is the difficulty of traviling without a Pilot. Found good wood, water, and grass about at our camp traviled 11 miles. Cold wind.

Sept. 10. Saturday very cold morning. Horses far from camp. Started at 8oclock found good places for camping which we might have come to last night. Commenced rising gradually at 10 oclock continued to rise until 12 when we came to a tremendous hill to descend. The mountains on our left were close by they rose gradualy and were covered with Pine Trees. Our descent lasted for near an hour, about midway of the hill was a little water course crossing our path & afforded us a resting place around this place were several Pine Trees. I noticed the White Pine and the Spruce Pine. Some were very tall & slim. From this little grove down the hill was more difficult all were obliged to dismount for safety. It was very sidling and uncomfortable rocky. Below was a most beautiful valley as I ever saw. We found good grass, a delightful road, &a fertile country in the valley, we crossed some small water courses and camp on a beautiful Creek at 3 o'clock good grass, & water & an abundance of wood traviled 20 miles found several well beaten trails leading from camp but none appeared fresh. After dark two Indians came to camp on horseback. They were of a different tribe from any which we had seen. They had traps and appeared to have been out but a short time. They told us that we could get to Wala Wala [sic Walla Walla, Oregon Territory] in 3 days.

Sept. 11. Sunday started at 7-1/2 o'clock with our Indians for Guide. They took us a northern direction & put us on the companies trail about 10 o'clock we then came to the Creek which we had left in the morning and followed it down. We discovered a band of Horses on the other side of the Creek. Our Indians left us about noon and crossed the Creek to these Horses which were being driven in the same direction we were going. We saw more Horses ahead. Came to an Indian village at 2 o'clock and camped near them, traviled 18 miles.

The first thing to be attended to after we camped was to assertain whether we could get any provisions from the Indians. We found to our great joy they had pleanty and instead of starving as we expected

25

we were able to trade enough fish to last us to Dr. Whitmans.* There were several lodges & they were well clad & had hundreds of good horses and an abundance of provision. I have seen no Indians since I started which appear so happy & well provided for as these. The beneficial influence of the Missionary Society appears to have reached here. They attended morning and evening devotion in our camp.

Marcus and Narcissa Whitman were early Christian missionaries at Walla Walla. They were killed by a band of Cayuse and Umatilla Indians along with eleven others on November 29, 1847.

12 Sept. Monday. Horses strayed far from camp and scattered among the Indians' Horses. The Indians showed moral honesty by bringing horses to us which had strayed by themselves to some distance. Started at 9-1/2 o'clock several Indians started with us one continued & said he would go to Dr. Whitmans. Commenced raising a Mountain by degrees. Came to trees, at first quite thin & without underbrush having fine grass. But as we arose we came to a densly timbered country, mostly pine & fir. The most beautiful tall straight trees. Our traviling through the timber was quite difficult ns the path wound back and forth and many logs lay across it. We decended & arose a tremendous hill and about 3 o'clock our Indian Guide beckoned us to take a by path to find water, we did so and after traveling a few hundred yards found a little opening of timber & pleanty of good water & some grass. Camped here for the night trav. 10 miles. Cool & cloudy considerable of rain after dark. Horses got frightened tied some up & the rest remained near.

Sept. 13 Tuesday. Started at 8-1/2 and followed back our path until we came to the main trail when we pusued our dismal rout, Our path today led through more dense places & driving our pack animals & cattle was almost impossible. Occasionally we found a clear spot frequently several acres together and in the forenoon several little springs of water, towards evening we left the timber and found ourselves on a rolling Prairie of good soil. Continued to deceud until near sunset when to our great joy we found water and wood but poor grass. Camped traviled 20 miles.

Sept. 14. Our Indian Guide told us we would get to Dr. Whitman's today but we hardly expected it as our animals were very much jaded. But it was nearer than we expected and we 'arrived at 3 o'clock and camped near his house traviled 8 m.

Dr. Whitman is a Missionary of the Presbyterian Order he has been in the Country six years. He has a very comfortable house and is farming to a considerable extent. He has a Thrashing Machine & a grinding mill all under one roof driven by waterpower. Many Indians around him. I was never more pleased to see a house or white people in my life, we were treated by Dr and Mrs. Whitman with the utmost kindness. We got what provision we wanted on very reasonable terms. I have just heard of the Death of young man who started from Independence with us. He was with the Hudson Bays Company and got drowned himself and horse crossing the Snake River soon after he left us. What is to me remarkable it was his gun and by an accident of his hand that put an end to poor Baily at Independence Rock. A small detachment, Forces', from the hind company came up.

Sept. 15. Having rec'd very bad treatment from the Indians we concluded to get away from here as soon as possible & try to find more grass, some of our company started before noon but we could not get ready until 3-1/2 oclock when we started down about 4 miles and found the rest of our company camped in an excelent spot. Forces came up also after dark.

Sept. 16. Started at 8 oclock kept down the Walawala [Walla Walla] River and camped at 1 o'clock within 3 miles of the Fort. Traviled 12 miles. Visited the Fort saw Esqr Crocker, Doct. White had left before noon in the Companies Boat.

All the foremost company had gone by land except Esqr. & Moss who started this evening to overtake them. I had an introduction to Mr. McKenlv who is in charge at the fort. The Fort is rebuilding now having lately been burnt. It is situated on a miserable sandy barren place where the sand drifts with the wind like snow. The Walla Walla River emties in & forms the Columbia here.

17. Sept. Saturday started at 9 o'clock drove to the Fort found Mr. McKenly from home not to return until evening could not get the Doct's Things drove down the river and camped, traveled four miles. The rest of the company went oh. The Banks of the River on each side present tremendous pinacles of rock mostly perpendicular. We find considerable of sage yet in places.

Sept. 18. Sunday. Went to the Fort before breakfast and got our things. Started at 9 o'clock lost two animals went back and found [them] and kept down the river, the most of time a steep bluff of rocks was on our left with occasional spots of grass sufficient for camping purposes stopped three hours for dinner, much sand and frequently in large drifts camped near sunset, traveled 12 m.

Sept. 19. Started at 8 a'clock drove on at a good pace very warm day camped in a good spot on the river traveled 15 m.

Sept. 20. Started at 8 o'clock kept down the river very sandy barren country destitute of timber (crossed the Unadilla). Cold wind & little rain. Mr. Spaulding & Lady over took us at noon rain increased. Camped at 4 o'clock, traviled 18 miles. Considerable rain. Cleared off before bed time. Mr. Gray called at camp on his return from Vancouver.

Started at 10 o'clock and parted with Mr. & Mrs. Spalding who in consequence of some intelligence from Mr. Gray resolved to return. Cold wind. Camped at 5 o'clock, traviled 20 miles.

Started late, cold wind, bad road, traviled 18 miles.

Started late, tremenndous west wind, lost my horse last night, Indians brought him into camp this morning, very rocky road over steep sidling places, crossed a large creek about noon. Camped at 4 o'clock. Traviled 11 miles.

24th Sept. Started very late, tremendous west wind & sand drifting like snow in our faces, passed over some large drifts. Came to a tremendous rapid Creek, obliged to take all our effects over in a canoe which was dangerous. Passed tremendous rocky falls in the River. Large Indian town, traveled 6 m.

25 Sept. Sunday, I feel bad this morning in consequence of getting wet yesterday and my eyes are much affected by the flying sand. Started at 11 o'clock traviled over hills & sidling places, saw a high snowy peak w'hicli we understand to be Mt. Hood. Passed the Dalis or rapids of the river which is a singular sight. Arrived at Mt. Perkins at 3 o'clock, found our old company there, traviled 8 miles. Mr. Perkins preached in camp this evening.

Visited Mr. Perkins at his house. Was very kindly rec'd and hospitably treated, got potatoes &c *and* started at I o'clock with an Indian Guide, rose a long hill and left the river, traviled over the most romantic country I have yet seen. The day is very pleasant indeed and the tall trees through which we are passing adds much to the beauty of the prospect. On our left arises Mt. Hood with its snowy peak glistening in the sunbeams, on the right & about the same distance Mt. Helena which resembles Mt. Hood very much. As we descended towards evening we saw far below us the river flowing as it were & dividing the two snowy peaks. We descended a considerable of a hill and found the pleasantest camp, the best wood, grass, and water we have had in a long time, travilled 12 miles started early arose and decended several rocky hills. Camped in the woods very little grass indeed, traviled 11 m.

Started at 8, got behind on account of a mule being lost. Our company left us. We started at 9 o'clock, missed one of our Indian horses but I thought he was with the other company. We came to a very rapid river just as they were across, very difficult crossing on account of large rocks and deep water, almost impossible to get along up the steep hills over the rocks & between the trees. Caught up with the company at 11 o'clock, found my horse not there started back to find him, found him at the camp we left had much difficulty to get him along. Two Indians overtook me at the river on my return with 5 good horses. I traviled with then' until dark when we came to an Indian Camp where we concluded to sleep. I got a few berries and a little fish for my supper. I crossed several rapid streams flowing from those snowy mountains before I got to Camp where I slept. We found no grass for our horses at all, traviled 13 miles.

Arose early after a very uncomfortable night's rest having only one blanket and a piece of Robe. My horses looked so bad I got one of the Indians horses to ride, started early without eating a particle, found the road horrible beyond description, met John Force soon who said he had lost 2 horses & was in search. The company had all tied up their horses to trees except the two that he had lost. He returned with us and gave up the search, overtook the rear of the company about 10 o'clock. One of our mules had been lost the day before while I was gone back for the horse. The horse I went back after gave o ut from hunger & fatigue, being very poor, and I was obliged to leave him in the woods, traviled along all day over hills and precipices, rocks and mire holes, over logs and under trees and across rapid streams, until at sunset we found a very little grass not worth mentioning & camped, traviled 20 miles. I found my apetite very good having eat very little in 36 hours.

Started early, found our animals very hollow and weak, passed down and crossed the stream found considerable grass in 2 miles from camp, traviled on until 11 o'clock when we stopped to bait our animals which were starving, started at I and drove on over as bad and some worse roads than ever, having frequent mire holes with logs in them, traviled up and down long hills and stopped at dark with very little grass and the most dismal & unpleasant camp I ever saw, traviled 13 miles.

Sunday, October 1st, 1842. My horse cannot be found this morning, 3 out of 5 of our riding animals give out so we have to start on foot. Starting at 8-1/2 found my horse on the way, horid road, logs& mud holes. Doct. Whites American mare very near giving out, found some grass and stopped at noon, traviled 5 miles. Concluded to stay here tonight.

Oct. 2, Sunday. Started at 9 o'clock some bad road met 3 of the young men who went down first, arrived at their camp at 4-1/2 o'clock, good grass and water, traviled 16 miles.

3d. A few of us accompanied those who were here before us to the Falls of Willamut where we found many people & considerable of buisness. Saw Dr. White & others who arrived before us, we were handsomely reed and kindly treated.

Packed up and started at 9 oclock called at the Falls and took dinner, found some of the men who came over with us at work on a mill. Mr. Jones & a man by name of Cooke much injured by blasting rocks, drove on and overtook our pack. Camped on a Creek. Traviled 10 miles.

Started at 9-1/2 crossed several streams, bad road. Camped in the settlements at the house of a Frenchman who treated us very kindly, traviled 10 m.

October 6. Started late took a round about road arrive at the mission at 2 o'clock, traviled 10 miles. Oct. 7. Rode about to see the country like it much. This is among the first frosty nights.

Went to the mill with Mrs. & Miss Brown. Mr. Benitt and Pomeroy together with several young men arrived in the settlement.

Sunday. Attended church twice today. Oct. 10. Mr. Pomeroy returned to the Falls. I crossed the River to see the country, stayed all night with Mr. O'Neil. 11. Rainy morning cleared off soon. Crossed the River & stayed all night at the Doct. House. 12. Clear fine weather. 13. Went with Mr. Shortess & Doct. Babcock to Youngs valley. Beautiful country, returned and wrote to my Father. 14. Commenced working a little. 18. Oct. Rainy morning cloudy day. 19. Oct. Rainy morning, cloudy & thick mist. 20. Rainy morning, cloudy day & some rain, rainy night. 21. Cloudy morning and day.

THE END

Discover more lost history from BIG BYTE BOOKS